CHEETAHS

BIG CATS

BY TAMMY GAGNE

Consultant: Christina Simmons
San Diego Zoo Global
San Diego, California

CAPSTONE PRESS
a capstone imprint

Edge Books are published by Capstone Press,
1710 Roe Crest Drive, North Mankato, Minnesota 56003.
www.capstonepub.com

Library of Congress Cataloging-in-Publication Data
Gagne, Tammy.
  Cheetahs / by Tammy Gagne.
    p. cm. – (Edge books. Big cats)
  Includes bibliographical references and index.
  ISBN 978-1-4296-7641-0 (library binding)
  1. Cheetah—Juvenile literature. I. Title.
  QL737.C23G34 2012
  599.75'9—dc22   2011010825

Summary: "Describes the history, physical features, and habitat of cheetahs" —
Provided by publisher.

Editorial Credits
Brenda Haugen, editor; Kyle Grenz, designer; Svetlana Zhurkin,
    media researcher; Laura Manthe, production specialist

Photo Credits
Alamy: Stock Connection Blue, 22–23; Corbis: Joe McDonald, 12; Creatas, 10,
28–29; Digital Stock, 1, 6; Dreamstime: Keith Wheatley, 15, Neal Cooper, 9,
Uros Ravbar, 26; Image Ideas, 24; Nature Picture Library: Christophe Courteau,
4; Shutterstock: BlueOrange Studio, 25, David W. Hughes, 14, Eric Isselée, 11,
Francois van Heerden, 21, Gail Johnson, 20, geraldb, 5, Jason Prince, 19 (top),
javarman, 13, 18–19, Justin Black, cover, Olga Khoroshunova, 7, photobar, 17,
Stanislav Eduardovich Petrov (background), throughout, thoron, 27, tigerbarb,
16–17

Printed in the United States of America in Stevens Point, Wisconsin.
102011   006404WZS12

TABLE OF CONTENTS

Chapter 1

SEEING SPOTS

From the top of a termite mound, the cheetah spots an impala. Before the impala even realizes it is being chased, the cheetah is right behind it. The African grasslands are a blur as the **prey** tries to outrun its hunter. Running at her top speed, the cheetah is almost out of energy. But she has cubs to feed, and the impala is tiring too. The cheetah holds on and wins the race.

- **4 million years ago –** The earliest known cheetahs lived.

- **About 10,000 years ago –** Cheetahs disappeared from North America.

- **About 3000 BC –** The ancient Sumerians became the first people to tame cheetahs.

- **About 1322 BC –** Artifacts with cheetah designs were buried in King Tutankhamen's tomb in Egypt.

- **AD 1300s to 1500s –** European princes and other nobles hunted with trained cheetahs.

- **AD 1556 to 1605 –** Akbar the Great of India owned more than 9,000 cheetahs during his reign.

Big Cat Fact

No two cheetahs have the same spot design.

At first glance, cheetahs look a lot like leopards. Both of these big cats have yellowish tan bodies and black spots. But cheetahs are much slimmer than leopards. Cheetahs also have black stripes that look like tear marks running from the corners of their eyes. These marks help reduce some of the glare from the sun.

Another way to identify a cheetah is by looking at its tail. All cheetahs have several black rings near the ends of their tails. The very end of the tail has a white tuft of fur.

prey–an animal hunted by another animal for food

BUILT FOR SPEED

Perhaps the only thing more amazing than the cheetah's beauty is its speed. The cheetah is the fastest **mammal** in the world. It can reach speeds of 60 miles (96 kilometers) an hour in just three seconds. But it can't keep up this extreme pace for long. It usually runs at top speed for about 300 yards (274 meters). Running this fast uses a lot of energy, and the cheetah tires quickly.

The cheetah was built for speed. Its body is long and narrow. A cheetah stands about 36 inches (91 centimeters) tall at the shoulder. It weighs about 75 pounds (34 kilograms). It has a small head for an animal of its size. These **traits** create less wind resistance when the cheetah runs.

mammal—a warm-blooded animal that breathes air and has hair or fur; female mammals feed milk to their young

trait—a quality or characteristic that makes one person or animal different from another

The cheetah is the only cat that has its claws exposed at all times. The claws give the animal better grip when running. The cat's long legs also take huge strides. These traits add to a cheetah's speed.

A cheetah's powerful tail can measure 30 inches (76 cm) long. The tail helps the big cat keep its balance. This is important when a cheetah must change direction while running.

Big Cat Fact

Cheetahs have whiskers, but they are much shorter than those of other big cats.

Size Comparison Chart

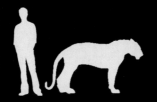

The average height of an American male is 5 feet, 10 inches (178 cm).

AT HOME

Cheetahs live in the African grasslands, dense and open woodlands, and semi-desert areas. They can be found east to west from Somalia to Senegal and as far south as northern South Africa. A small number of cheetahs live in southern Algeria and northern Niger. They also live in Iran, which is in Asia.

Cheetahs are not as strong as other animals living in these areas. Lions, leopards, hyenas, and wild dogs can defeat a cheetah in a fight. Most cheetahs use their speed to avoid these animals.

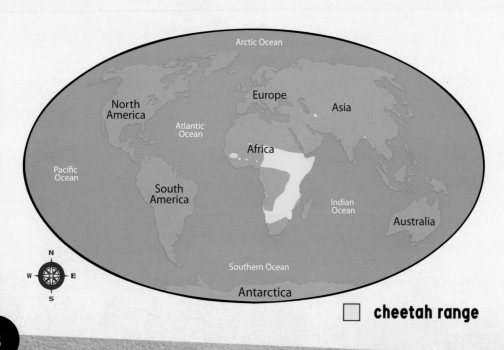

☐ **cheetah range**

More than 90 percent of wild cheetah cubs die before they reach adulthood. Other wild animals often snatch cubs when their mothers are away hunting. A cheetah that makes it to adulthood may live up to 12 years. Cheetahs in **captivity** may live as long as 17 years.

Chapter 2

ON THE PROWL

Cheetahs are meat eaters. They use their speed for hunting. These athletic cats can catch some of the fastest animals in Africa. Most cheetahs prefer to feast on small antelope, gazelles, and impalas. A cheetah can catch larger animals such as zebras and wildebeests. But the risk of losing a fight is greater with these larger animals.

Big Cat Fact

Cheetahs have no permanent homes or dens. They spend their lives roaming.

HUNTING HABITS

Female cheetahs hunt alone, except when teaching their cubs this important skill. When a female hunts alone, she grabs her prey and holds onto it until she has killed it. When she is teaching her cubs, a cheetah will grab the prey and release it. Then the younger cheetahs can practice making the kill.

Males are more likely to hunt in small groups called **coalitions**. By working together, male cheetahs are better able to hunt large prey.

coalition—a group of male cheetahs, usually brothers, that live and hunt together

A cheetah defends its kill against a smaller predator.

COMPETING FOR FOOD

Many African animals hunt at night and sleep during the day. Cheetahs do just the opposite. By hunting during the day, they have less competition for their food. Cheetahs in the north African Sahara have been seen hunting at night, though.

When another large **predator** arrives on the scene, a single cheetah will usually retreat. A hungry lion can weigh four times as much as a cheetah. This size difference makes defending the kill an unwise choice for the smaller cat. Instead, cheetahs focus on hiding their food from other animals. Cheetahs often drag their kills to shady, hidden places before they eat.

AVOIDING PREDATORS

An adult cheetah can usually get away from its predators. When a larger animal kills an adult cheetah, it's often because of a fight over food. Cheetah cubs that are left alone are often killed by lions, leopards, and hyenas.

Big Cat Fact

Cheetahs get most of their water from the meat they eat. If a cheetah is eating properly, it only needs to drink water once every three to four days.

predator—an animal that hunts other animals for food

Chapter 3

HIGHLY-TUNED SENSES

Cheetahs have great eyesight. This is the sense they rely on most when hunting. They can spy their prey from as far away as 3 miles (4.8 km). A cheetah will climb small hills or termite mounds each day to search for prey within this range.

Cheetahs cannot see as well at night as they can during the day. Poor nighttime vision is unusual for a cat. The cheetah's eyes have more **cones** and fewer **rods** than the eyes of other types of wildcats. This difference means that cheetahs may likely see more colors than other cats can.

Cheetahs also have a broad field of vision. Their eyesight covers a wide area. People can see objects within an area of 140 degrees, while a cheetah's eyesight covers an area of 210 degrees.

cone—cell in an animal's eye that helps it see color

rod—cell in an animal's eye that helps it see in low light

OTHER SENSES

Although they may have small ears, cheetahs have very sharp hearing. Cheetahs can detect sounds at very high **frequencies**. They can hear many sounds people cannot.

The black patches on the backs of a cheetah's ears look like eyes. This likeness protects the cat from predators. When another animal spots a cheetah from behind, it is less likely to attack if it thinks the cheetah sees it.

frequency—the number of sound waves that pass a location in a certain amount of time

Cheetahs use their noses to tell which hunting territories already belong to other cheetahs. Male cats claim certain areas as their own by marking trees and other objects with urine. Most other cheetahs will then avoid these places.

MAKING NOISE

Cheetahs don't roar like other big cats. When a cheetah wants to call another cheetah, it uses a high-pitched yip. When a cub tries to make this sound, it comes out sounding more like a bird's chirp. Cheetahs also growl or hiss to express annoyance or fear.

Big Cat Fact

Cheetahs are the only big cats that purr.

BRINGING UP BABIES

Male and female cheetahs lead different lives. Males are social. They bond strongly with the members of their coalitions. They usually live and hunt with these other cats for life. Female cheetahs are loners. When they do not have cubs to care for, females live alone.

Many animals give birth in the spring, but cheetahs can have cubs any time during the year. Once a mother has a litter, she won't have any more cubs until after the first litter is living on its own. Cheetah cubs live with their mother for about a year and a half.

But many cheetah cubs die before they reach adulthood. Sometimes other animals, such as lions or baboons, kill cheetah cubs. Other times the mother cheetah cannot find enough food for her litter. If all the cubs die, a cheetah will often have another litter much sooner. A female cheetah often has between four and six litters during her lifetime.

Female cheetahs become more social when it is time to mate. When the cubs are born, the mother cares for them. Father cheetahs play no role in bringing up their young.

WELCOME TO THE WORLD

Cheetahs give birth to litters of between one and eight cubs. A newborn cheetah has a long furry coat called a mantle. This bushy fur can make a cub look bigger and less helpless to predators. It also helps the animal blend into its surroundings. Cubs shed most of their mantle over the next few months as their spotted coats grow in.

Big Cat Fact

Some scientists believe a cub's mantle may also protect it from rain and hot temperatures.

A mother cheetah keeps her babies
hidden until they are five to six weeks old.
Mothers move their cubs every few days to
keep predators from finding them. A mother
must leave her cubs alone when she hunts.
At six weeks the cubs begin following her on
hunts and eating meat from her kills.

LIFE LESSONS

A female cheetah will spend the next year teaching her cubs to hunt for themselves. Cheetahs may back down to fights over food, but mothers will defend their cubs at all costs. A mother may even take on two male cheetahs if they threaten her young. Adult male cheetahs sometimes kill and eat cubs if the mother is not nearby.

Cheetahs in the Movies

The Disney movie *Cheetah* is based on the book *The Cheetahs* by Alan Caillou. The story centers on two teenage siblings who are unhappy when their family moves to Kenya. Life gets more interesting when they discover an orphaned cheetah. But then the cat is stolen. A young goat herder joins in their efforts to rescue the animal.

Cubs stay with their mothers until they are about a year and a half old. After their mother leaves, the cubs stay together for at least six more months. Around this time the males form coalitions and go off in search of their own territories. By the time female cheetahs are 2 years old, they are ready to start families of their own.

WILL THEY SURVIVE?

The cheetah is one of the most **endangered** cats in Africa. In the early 1900s, more than 100,000 cheetahs lived in Africa and Asia. Now the cats are nearly extinct in Asia. Less than 100 still live in Iran. About 15,000 wild cheetahs remain in Africa. Populations are highest in Namibia and Botswana.

One problem is overhunting, even though in most cases hunting cheetahs is against the law. The only way people can legally kill cheetahs is if the cats come onto their land and put humans or farm animals at risk.

Many cheetahs are killed for their spotted skins. **Poachers** don't care about these deaths. They only care about the money they get from selling the skins.

OTHER ISSUES

Another problem is that so few cubs survive in the wild. Animal predators pose a big threat to a cub's survival. But we must consider why there are so many predators.

More and more people are moving into the areas where cheetahs and other animals live. These people are using large amounts of land for farming. The wild animals are being forced to share smaller areas of land. This habitat loss increases competition for the same food.

Wildlife reserves try to provide endangered animals with land where they will be safe from poachers. This strategy works for many animals, but cheetahs are different. Other predators still cause problems for the cheetahs. Larger predators steal cheetahs' kills and kill cheetahs' young. Many cheetahs are just as endangered within the reserves as they are outside them.

TRYING TO HELP

Several groups are working to help save cheetahs. The Cheetah Conservation Fund is teaching people in Africa how to protect their livestock without killing cheetahs. Dogs called Anatolian shepherds can be trained to guard the farmers' livestock. If farmers keep and train these dogs, the farmers won't need to kill cheetahs. This plan could be the cheetahs' best hope for survival.

Big Cat Fact

The Serengeti Cheetah Project began in 1974. Back then its goal was to learn more about cheetahs. Today it focuses almost completely on conservation.

You Can Help Too

Did you know that you can adopt a cheetah through the World Wildlife Fund (WWF)? Of course you can't take the cheetah home with you. But your adoption fee helps support the WWF's programs to protect the cheetah and its wild habitat.

GLOSSARY

captivity (kap-TIV-ih-tee)—the condition of being kept in a cage

coalition (koh-uh-LISH-uhn)—a group of male cheetahs, usually brothers, that live and hunt together

cone (KOHN)—a cell in an animal's eye that helps it see color

endangered (en-DAYN-juhrd)—at risk of dying out

frequency (FREE-kwuhn-see)—the number of sound waves that pass a location in a certain amount of time

mammal (MAM-uhl)—a warm-blooded animal that breathes air and has hair or fur; female mammals feed milk to their young

poacher (POHCH-ur)—a person who hunts or fishes illegally

predator (PRED-uh-tur)—an animal that hunts other animals for food

prey (PRAY)—an animal hunted by another animal for food

rod (RAHD)—a cell in an animal's eye that helps it see in low light

trait (TRATE)—a quality or characteristic that makes one person or animal different from another

READ MORE

Becker, John E. *Frenemies for Life: Cheetahs and Anatolian Shepherd Dogs.* Columbus, Ohio: Columbus Zoo and Aquarium, 2010.

Hansen, Rosanna. *Caring for Cheetahs: My African Adventure.* Honesdale, Penn.: Boyd Mills Press, 2007.

Johns, Chris, with Elizabeth Carney. *Face to Face with Cheetahs.* Washington, D.C.: National Geographic, 2008.

INTERNET SITES

FactHound offers a safe, fun way to find Internet sites related to this book. All of the sites on FactHound have been researched by our staff.

Here's all you do:

Visit *www.facthound.com*

Type in this code: 9781429676410

Super-cool stuff! Check out projects, games and lots more at
www.capstonekids.com

INDEX